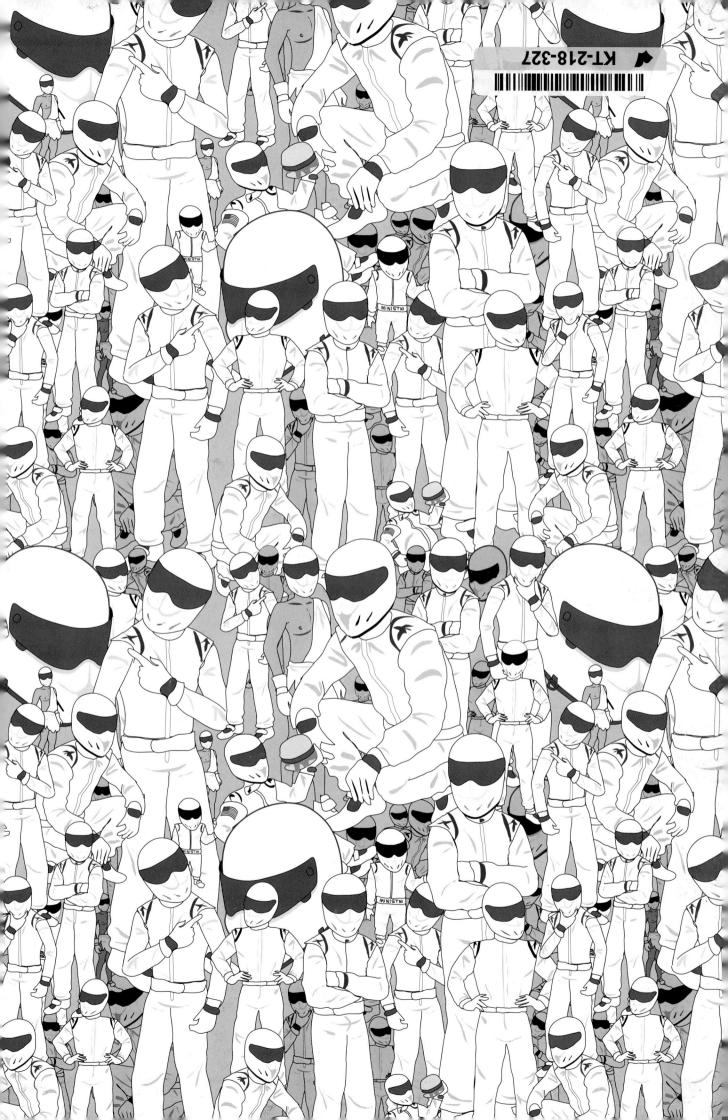

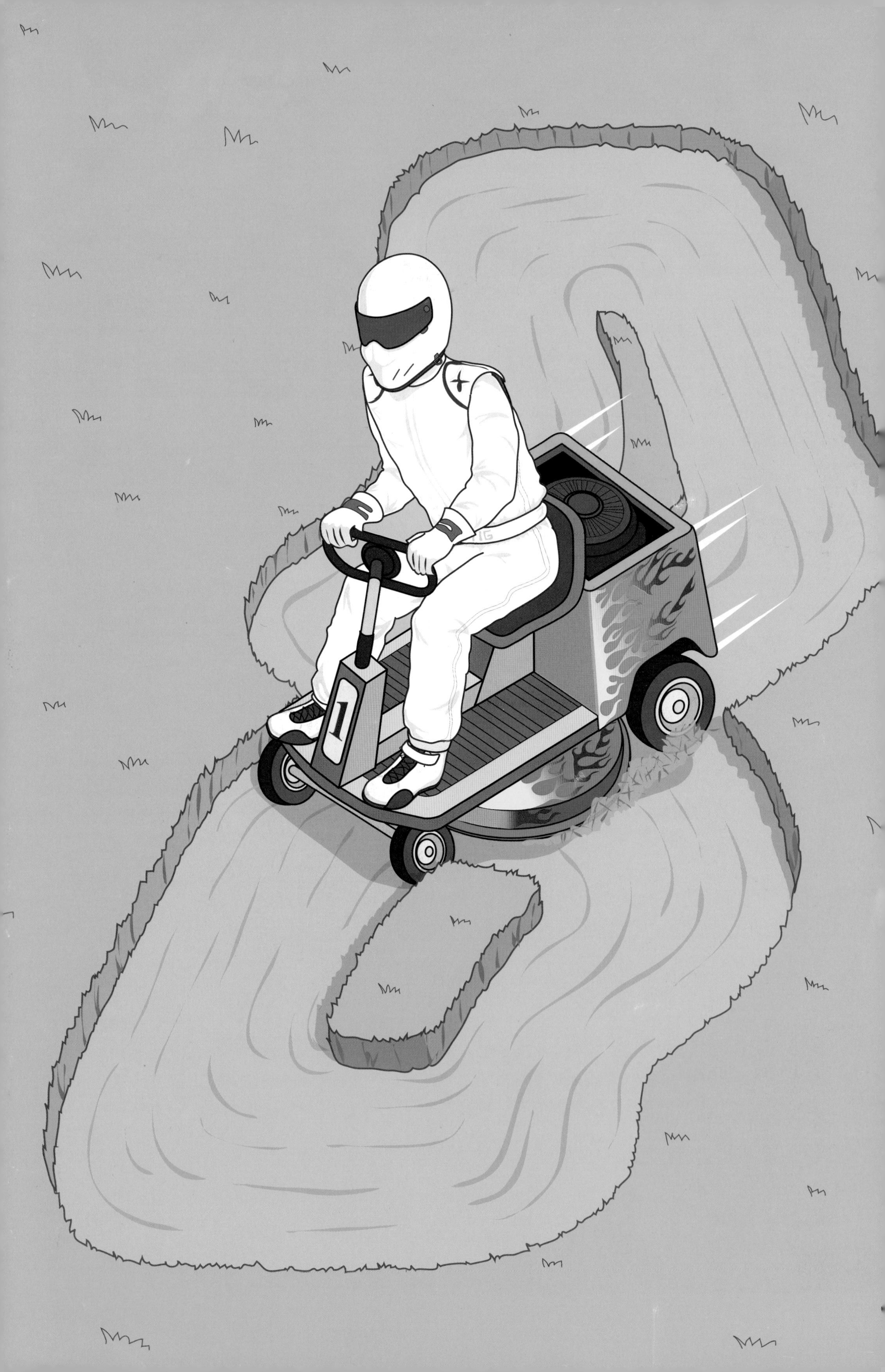

TopGear

'Where's Stig?'

Illustrations by Rod Hunt
Words by Matt Master

BBC BOOKS

Contents

HERE'S WHAT YOU NEED TO FIND IN EVERY SCENE

Stig

Jeremy

Richard

James

The Producer

Challenge Man

Top Gear Dog

Stuntman

Ghost of Black Stig

Spam

Dynamite

Bumper Dumper

Fuel

Stig Jam

Stig Sarnie

Dunsfold Map

Stig's Raw Meat

Biscuits

No Caravans

Oil

Dacia Sandero Model

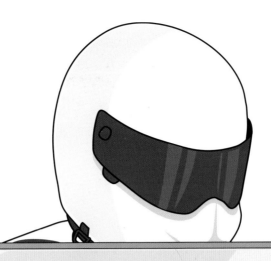

Welcome to Where's Stig?

The super-secretive existence of our favourite socially dysfunctional motoring automaton is under threat.

A reluctance to speak, combined with a surgical sense-of-humour bypass and a severe physical allergy to Ant and Dec, has always demanded he shun the limelight. But now, with the international paparazzi scrabbling to unmask him and every speed freak in Christendom determined to prove it's only Damon Hill under that visor, The Stig is committed to going underground.

Time for you to search for The Stig and a few other familiar characters in the far-flung corners of our nameless, faceless hero's adoptive planet, while he keeps a watchful eye on the unimaginable incompetence of his so-called colleagues. Good luck! Keep your eyes peeled and your wits about you.

Who knows where
The Stig might end up?

The Studio

Even in the place he's reluctantly learnt to call home, it's impossible to get a moment's peace and quiet for a hot cup of 95 Ron and a cigarette. Much more of this and there'll be more than one ex-Stig memorial outside the studio.

Botswana

It's a jungle out there and no place for a faceless driving demi-god in a Nomex jump suit and crash helmet. Particularly not when your sweat smells of competition-grade engine oil and you have to carry your preferred liquid refreshment in a jerry can.

Vietnam

Wholly unimpressed by a national obsession with single-cylinder single bhp scooters, our favourite unearthly entity is determined to find Vietnam's other fastest form of transport. How else to escape hippy backpackers and stray extras from *Apocalypse Now*?

The North Pole

Concerned by some stuff in the papers, *Top Gear* has driven a massive red pick-up truck to the North Pole to see if the ice cap really is melting and Stig's reputation has preceded him. The locals have already sculpted a snowstig in his honour. Now here's a place where The Stig can take full advantage of his natural camouflage. At least until Jeremy has single-handedly thawed out the Arctic.

Yes really, it's the **North Pole**

The Deep South

From the frozen North to the deep, and deeply sweaty, South, Stig is lying exceedingly low while the boys bait the locals. Someone's going to end up dead, or worse, in a communal jail cell. But in a land where prams have V8s and wars are waged for a tank of gasoline, he's actually feeling right at home.

Tokyo

It's easy to disappear in a city where weirdness is a pastime, where wandering around in a white jump suit, having no genitalia and a phobia of ducks doesn't warrant a second glance. This is the land of competitive drifting after all, the modifier's Mecca, where even the trains break the sound barrier. It's almost tempting to put down some roots.

Stigs in Space

Meanwhile, in deep space, the top secret cloning experiments seem to be going remarkably well. It won't be long before Earth is overrun with a million identical Stig minions. And their overlord can hardly wait for a colony of like-minded mute, humourless, speed-addled sociopaths. But remember, unlike his protégés, The Stig wouldn't be seen dead with his nipples on show.

Costa del Stig

Anonymity is proving hard to come by on the teeming beaches of the Costa Dole Queue. Lobster-pink bodies blister under the Spanish sun as the only figure wearing gloves and boots in a forty degree heatwave hunts desperately for some shade and a cooling half of Optimax. Definitely time to move on.

Bonneville Salt Flats

Things are looking up. Granted it's twice as hot as the Costa, but at least the sole purpose for getting sweaty out here is the search for ungodly speed. For a desert there sure are a lot of faces, but it's not going to be hard to blend in amongst these suicidal nitrous junkies. They have so much in common.

Stig's Secret Bunker

Away from prying eyes for a while, and a chance to catch up on Stig Inc.'s latest developments, and dwarf henchman, Mini-Stig. The suits are coming up whiter than white at long last, but the sharks are getting hungry. Perhaps it's time to invite the Minister for Transport over for a dip...

The English Channel

Ah, the busiest shipping lane on the planet. What better place to take refuge from a world hell-bent on revealing Stig's identity? There's not much for a motor-racing monolith to do on the high seas, but he can always daydream about the prospect of Jeremy falling overboard to keep his spirits up.

Festival Stig

Amazing what passes for entertainment in these parts. Still, another crowd is another place to hide, at least until he can make it back to his tent. The burger may have been a mistake though, what with the size of the queue for the bog. Perhaps there's somewhere a Stig can squat unnoticed, but it's going to be tricky to get that suit off.

Checklist
Yet more stuff to try and find

The Studio

- ❏ Fiat 500 Abarth
- ❏ Pagani Zonda F Roadster
- ❏ Bugatti Veyron
- ❏ Ariel Atom
- ❏ Mercedes McLaren SLR
- ❏ Caterham R500
- ❏ Ferrari 360
- ❏ Lotus Exige
- ❏ Maserati MC12
- ❏ TVR T350
- ❏ Nissan GT-R
- ❏ London taxi
- ❏ Crash-test dummies
- ❏ *Top Gear* police car
- ❏ Learn Morse Code book
- ❏ *Golden Girls* poster
- ❏ *Top Gear* chef
- ❏ Aquada
- ❏ Gambon
- ❏ Jay Kay
- ❏ Simon Cowell
- ❏ Gordon Ramsay
- ❏ Hugh Grant
- ❏ Jamie Oliver
- ❏ Ewan McGregor
- ❏ Billie Piper
- ❏ Justin Hawkins
- ❏ Simon Pegg
- ❏ Mark Wahlberg
- ❏ David Tennant
- ❏ Will Young
- ❏ Ronnie Wood
- ❏ Jools Holland
- ❏ Ray Winstone
- ❏ Keith Allen
- ❏ Tom Jones
- ❏ Dame Helen Mirren
- ❏ Kristin Scott Thomas
- ❏ Boris Johnson
- ❏ Brian Cox
- ❏ Ellen MacArthur
- ❏ Chris Evans
- ❏ Paul McKenna
- ❏ Roger Daltrey
- ❏ Patrick Stewart
- ❏ Carol Voderman

- ❏ Christian Slater
- ❏ Joanna Lumley
- ❏ Jordan
- ❏ Eddie Izzard
- ❏ Stephen Fry
- ❏ David Soul
- ❏ Geri Halliwell
- ❏ Johnny Vegas
- ❏ Ian McKellan

Botswana

- ❏ VW Beetle
- ❏ Ford Escort MK1
- ❏ BMW 2002
- ☑ Stig's African cousin
- ☑ The very dangerous Honey Badger (with someone's testicles)
- ❏ Botswanan Vice President
- ❏ Bush mechanic
- ❏ Comb-over man
- ☑ Rhinos
- ☑ Two guys in red ties

Vietnam

- ❏ Commie Stig
- ❏ Stars & Stripes bike
- ❏ Francis Ford Coppola
- ❏ Medallion man
- ☑ Biker transporting pigs
- ☑ Megaphone man
- ❏ Colander helmet
- ❏ Man with a hoe
- ☑ Bikini cocktail girl
- ☑ Pink scooter lady
- ❏ Vietnamese test track
- ❏ Binocular man

The North Pole

- ❏ Jack Frost
- ❏ Snowman Stig
- ❏ The Abominable Snowman
- ❏ James's spam
- ❏ Skier
- ❏ Ice sculpture
- ❏ UFO

- ❏ G&Ts
- ❏ Royal Navy
- ❏ Man with snowshoes
- ❏ Emergency fine wines

Deep South

- ❏ 2 Hummers
- ❏ Chrysler PT Cruiser
- ❏ 2 GMC Yukons
- ❏ Jeep
- ❏ 1967 Cadillac DeVille
- ☑ Stig's fat American cousin
- ☑ Hick swimming pool
- ☑ Hick swing
- ☑ Peeing man
- ☑ Dead rabbit
- ❏ Butler
- ❏ New Orleans band
- ☑ BBQ hick
- ☑ Old man on lawnmower
- ❏ Angry garage woman
- ❏ Drunk man sleeping
- ☑ No Hunting sign
- ☑ Hick brawl
- ❏ Mexican fruit pickers

Tokyo

- ❏ Toyota RiN
- ❏ Mitsuoka Orochi
- ❏ Mitsuoka Galue
- ❏ Honda PUYO
- ❏ Nissan Pivo
- ❏ Samurai
- ❏ Punk girl
- ☑ Asimo robot
- ❏ Dude with pink scarf
- ☑ Woman in mouse suit
- ☑ Karaoke singers
- ☑ Sumo wrestlers
- ❏ Dapper bow-tie man
- ☑ Sexy emo babe
- ☑ Stig advert
- ☑ Woman in music dress
- ☑ Funky guy in stripy suit
- ❏ Girl with heart-shaped pendant
- ☑ Mount Fuji poster

- ❏ Polka dot girl
- ❏ Bullet train
- ❏ Japanese Heidi

Stigs in Space
- ❏ Stig-o-matics
- ❏ Space hoppers
- ❏ Trooper with hammer
- ❏ Chef trooper
- ❏ Painter troopers
- ❏ Trooper with roll of cable
- ❏ Troopers on the throne
- ❏ Darth Stig
- ❏ Monolith
- ❏ Meteor
- ❏ Welding trooper
- ❏ Trooper with wrench
- ❏ Trooper in underpants
- ❏ Surfing troopers
- ❏ UFO
- ❏ Rear view mirrors
- ❏ Troopers with solar panel

Costa del Stig
- ❏ Zonda F
- ❏ Ford GT
- ❏ Ferrari F430 Spider
- ❏ Beach Buggy
- ❏ Mini Moke
- ❏ VW Camper
- ❏ Aston Martin DB9
- ❏ HMS Stig
- ❏ Mooning man
- ❏ Nice cup of tea
- ❏ Bald bare-chested man
- ❏ Dreadhead
- ❏ Zimmer frame lady
- ❏ Number 1 surfer
- ❏ La policia
- ❏ Drunk Scotsman
- ❏ DJ
- ❏ Inflatable armchair
- ❏ Naked man
- ❏ Naked woman
- ❏ Flamenco guy
- ❏ Man in bikini
- ❏ Man puking

- ☑ Couple snogging
- ☑ Learner surfer
- ☑ Muscle men
- ☑ Beer-gut cameraman
- ☑ Guy who's wet himself
- ☑ Jaws

Bonneville Salt Flats
- ❏ Green Monster
- ❏ Caddy CTS-V
- ❏ Bluebird
- ❏ Golden Arrow
- ❏ Craig Breedlove's Spirit of America (3 different ones)
- ❏ Dodge Challenger
- ❏ Thrust
- ❏ Thrust SSC
- ❏ Bloodhound
- ❏ BAR F1
- ❏ Golden Rod
- ❏ JCB DieselMax
- ❏ MG EX181
- ❏ Corvette ZR1
- ❏ Cowboy couple
- ❏ Hunter S Thompson
- ❏ Car 101
- ❏ Biggles
- ❏ All-red racing driver
- ❏ Bruce Willis
- ❏ Fact police
- ❏ Too noisy for these people

Stig's Secret Bunker
- ❏ Mazda Furai
- ❏ Bugatti Veyron
- ❏ Koenigsegg
- ❏ KTM-X-Bow
- ❏ Lamborghini Murcielago
- ❏ Mini Stig
- ❏ Rubik's cube
- ❏ Angelina Jolie
- ❏ Fat henchman
- ❏ Ninjas
- ❏ Little Hamster
- ❏ Rocket pack henchmen
- ❏ Cleaner henchmen
- ❏ Butler henchman

- ❏ Golden woman
- ❏ Mincemeat-o-meter
- ❏ One-eyed henchman
- ❏ Bowler-hatted baddie
- ❏ Portrait of Stig
- ❏ Scientist with syringe
- ❏ *Evil Monthly* magazine

The English Channel
- ❏ Aquada
- ❏ Old lady in green hat
- ❏ David Walliams
- ❏ Lady in raspberry beret
- ❏ Beardy Branson
- ☑ Lady pirate
- ❏ Ellen MacArthur
- ❏ Vicar
- ❏ Suave smoker
- ❏ Ice cream

Festival Stig
- ☑ Man in Indian headress
- ☑ His n' hers goth couple
- ❏ Music police
- ❏ Vomiting man
- ❏ Foxy purple hair girl
- ☑ Stig's tent
- ☑ Guy in 'I'm the Stig' t-shirt
- ❏ Snogging couple
- ❏ Beetlesaurous car
- ❏ Jester
- ❏ Pink Mohican guy
- ❏ The Gallager brothers
- ❏ Jay Z
- ❏ PJ Harvey
- ❏ Slash
- ❏ U2
- ❏ Matt Bellamy from Muse
- ❏ Paul Weller
- ❏ Amy Winehouse
- ❏ Jack Black
- ❏ Katie White from Ting Tings
- ❏ Jarvis Cocker
- ❏ Prince
- ❏ Dave Grohl from Foo Fighters
- ❏ Mick Jagger

Acknowledgements

Rod Hunt would like to thank Derek Brazell & Becky Brown at the Association of Illustrators, Andrew Coningsby, Bee Willey and Russell Cobb & Charlie Turner at Top Gear.

10 9 8 7 6 5

Published in 2009 by BBC Books, an imprint of Ebury Publishing. A Random House Group Company

The Random House Group Limited Reg. No. 954009

Addresses for companies within the Random House Group can be found at www.randomhouse.co.uk

A CIP catalogue record for this book is available from the British Library.

ISBN 978 1 84 607808 8

The Random House Group Limited supports the Forest Stewardship Council (FSC), the leading international forest certification organisation. All our titles that are printed on Greenpeace approved FSC certified paper carry the FSC logo. Our paper procurement policy can be found at www.rbooks.co.uk/environment

Commissioning editor: Lorna Russell
Project editors: Caroline McArthur & Kelda Grant
Design and Creative Direction: Charlie Turner
Production: Antony Heller

Printed and bound in Italy by Graphicom Srl

To buy books by your favourite authors and register for offers, visit www.rbooks.co.uk

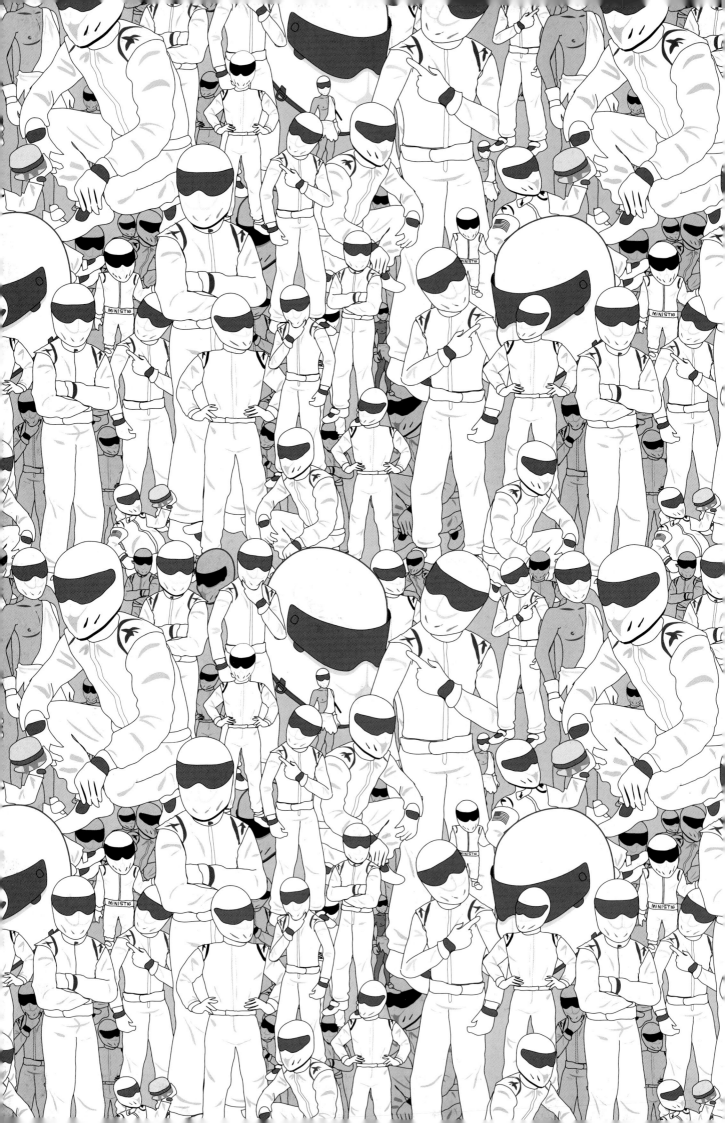